WOODCARVING A *Halloween* CHESS SET

Photo credits:

Dwayne Gosnell: 7, 48, and all step-by-step photos

Mike Mihalo: front and back cover, 2-3, 4-5, 6, 8, 9, 16-17, 18, 22, 26, 30, 32, 38, 44, and all photos of finished chess pieces

Courtesy Shutterstock:
FOTOKITA 16-17 (background); primopiano cover, 1, 4-5, 17 (wood background); YummyBuum 18, 22, 26, 32, 38, 44 (spider web)

ISBN 978-1-4971-0082-4

Library of Congress Control Number: 2020005480

To learn more about the other great books from Fox Chapel Publishing, or to find a retailer near you, call toll-free 800-457-9112 or visit us at *www.FoxChapelPublishing.com*.

We are always looking for talented authors. To submit an idea, please send a brief inquiry to acquisitions@foxchapelpublishing.com.

Printed in China
First printing

WOODCARVING A *Halloween* CHESS SET

PATTERNS AND INSTRUCTIONS FOR
Caricature Carving

Dwayne Gosnell

FOX CHAPEL
PUBLISHING

Contents

Acknowledgments

I want to extend my deepest thanks to everyone along the way who told me to keep carving and never give up.

Dedication

To my loving wife, Melissa, for always supporting me throughout the endless woodchips, and to my daughter and son for always being there to help make the funny funnier.

Before You Carve

Basic Carving Instructions

All you really need in order to carve is a space to complete your project, a comfy chair, some wood, and the carving tools of your choice. I've never met a carver who wasn't also a tool collector. If you have it, use it. If I use a certain tool in the instructions, but you can accomplish the same thing with a different tool, do it. Here are some points to remember:

- Make sure that your tools are as sharp as they can be. You shouldn't force dull tools into the wood.
- Carve as much as you can every day. Don't be afraid to challenge yourself.
- Don't carve while tired, as this can lead to miscuts—either in the wood or your hand.
- Always use protective gear, such as gloves and finger guards.
- Remember that everyone makes mistakes—it's only a block of wood! Don't expect to create a perfect carving right away; the fun is in the journey.

Getting Started

Just like in chess, you need to plan and think ahead when carving a chess set. Luckily, I have taken some of the planning out of it by providing a list to get you started (see page 8). All of the pieces are cut from 2" (5.1cm) square basswood stock. You will need a bandsaw or access to one due to the number of carvings. You can cut the pieces out with a coping saw, but with thirty-two pieces per chess set, it could take a while.

For expediency, I cut out all of the pieces in the set prior to carving.

Always protect your hands while carving. To keep your knife blade sharp, apply stropping compound to a piece of leather. Then, with the bevel facing away from you, pull the knife toward you across the stropping compound in a reverse shaving-type motion—you don't want the blade to dig into the leather.

Cutting Out the Blanks

1 Place the front and side patterns on the basswood blank. You can draw around the pattern (like I have done), attach the pattern with repositionable spray adhesive, or use graphite paper and a pencil to transfer the pattern onto the wood.

2 Cut the front view. Tape the waste wood back in place; this will provide stability and a reference point when cutting the adjacent view.

3 Cut the adjacent side.

4 Remove the blank from the waste wood. *Note: Take your time! Speed is not your friend in these steps. I used a ¼" (6mm)-wide blade with six TPI (teeth per inch); however, you could use a smaller blade if desired.*

Materials and Tools

MATERIALS:

- Basswood, 2" (5.1cm) square (quantities given are for one complete chess set):
  - Pawns: 16 blocks at 3¾" (9.5cm) tall
  - Rooks: 4 blocks at 4" (10cm) tall
  - Knights: 4 blocks at 4⅜" (11cm) tall
  - Bishops: 4 blocks at 4¾" (12cm) tall
  - Queens: 2 blocks at 5" (13cm) tall
  - Kings: 2 blocks at 5½" (14cm) tall
- Patterns and graphite paper, stylus, or pencil
- Carving glove: Your choice, but make sure that your carving glove fits snug to your hand. A loose carving glove will allow the tool to grab and possibly slice into your hand or fingers.

TOOLS:

I used the following tools to create the chess set. Feel free to use the tools you have available or what works best for you.

- Bandsaw (I use a ¼" [6mm] blade with six TPI [teeth per inch])
- Carving knife of choice
- Detail knife of choice
- Hole punch (eye punch), ¼" (6mm)
- 45° V-tool, ⅛" (3mm)
- 45° V-tool, ¼" (6mm)
- 90° V-tool, ½" (13mm)
- V-tool, soft, ⅜" (10mm)
- #7 gouge, ¾" (19mm)
- #9 gouge, ⅛" (3mm)
- #9 gouge, ¼" (6mm)

PAINT:

A paint chart is provided on page 17, with individual paint colors listed after each project.

PAINTBRUSHES:

I don't get picky about sizes, but make sure that you have quality brushes.

V-Tool Layers

Lay the V-tool on its side to create layers in wood easily. This helps separate clothing and prevents the need to make a lot of knife stops and relief cuts on your project. It also saves time; instead of having to make and carve up to a bunch of stop cuts, you can relieve certain areas in just one pass.

Artist's Loft
FolkArt
ACRYLIC PAINT
PEINTURE ACRYLIQUE
PINTURA ACRÍLICA
PLAID
2 fl oz 59 ml

Practice

Carving Eyes

Carving the eyes is easily the most stressful challenge to a carver of any skill level. After all, the eyes are the first thing that everyone sees when looking at a carving. However, with this easy approach, I hope to show you that carving eyes is nothing to be afraid of and can even be quite simple.

Practice carving eyes on a separate block of scrap wood prior to carving the project.

1 Start in the center of the upper eyelid, cutting toward the nose, with a ¼" (6mm) 45° V-tool. Then, with the same V-tool, complete the other half of the upper eyelid. If you find this V-tool too large, use a ⅛" (3mm) 45° V-tool instead.

2 With the V-tool you used in step 1, cut the lower part of the upper eyelid, which will be the eye opening. Then cut the lower eyelid to complete the eye opening.

3 With your favorite knife (I use a detail knife for eyes), carve a triangle-shaped chip on each side of the eyeball and then remove the chip cleanly. The lowest point of the chip should be closest to the edge of the eye, making the eyeball appear round.

4 Define the eyelids with the knife you used in step 3. This will create shadows, which add depth and interest to the eye area.

5 Using the same knife, spend a bit of time making the eyes round. The rounder the eye, the better it looks. Thin the upper eyelids. Make sure there are no hidden or hanging chips.

Steps 1-5

Carving Noses

The nose of any piece can set the tone for how the entire face will look. Will the nose be too small, too big, too thin, too flat? Calm down, my friend! Your nose will look great as long as you plan out what you want and stick to the plan. I start each nose by planning to carve it a bit bigger than needed—remember, we can't add wood back once it's gone.

Note: Think in flat planes for a simple approach, and use the tool that fits the carving; no sizes are exact.

1 Cut into the blank, carving upward from the tip of the nose with your carving knife (which you will use for all of these steps unless otherwise indicated). Then carve down to the deepest point of the first cut from the opposite side, creating a low area (valley). Remove the chip you just created.

2 Cut upward along the top right side of the valley and remove the chip as you did in step 1.

3 Cut upward along the top left side of the valley and remove the chip as you did in step 1.

4 Cut downward along the bottom of the tip of the nose. Remove the chip by cutting upward from the chin area.

5 On one side of the nose, cut downward and then remove the chip as you did in step 4.

6 On the other side of the nose, cut downward and then remove the chip as you did in step 4.

7 With a V-tool, carve the sides of the nose. Notice that the side of the tool closest to the nose follows the same angle as the nose. Do not cut straight into the nose.

8 With the knife, remove a triangle in the corner of the nose. This will round the bottom slightly.

9 Repeat the process in step 8 on the opposite side.

10 Deepen the bridge of the nose to create more of a profile.

11 With a gouge, remove the wood above the nostrils by carving upward to the eye area.

12 With the same tool, carve from the outside of the face inward, removing the chip. This creates the eye socket as well.

13 With the knife, carve shadow lines around the nostril. Again, do not undercut or cut straight into the nose.

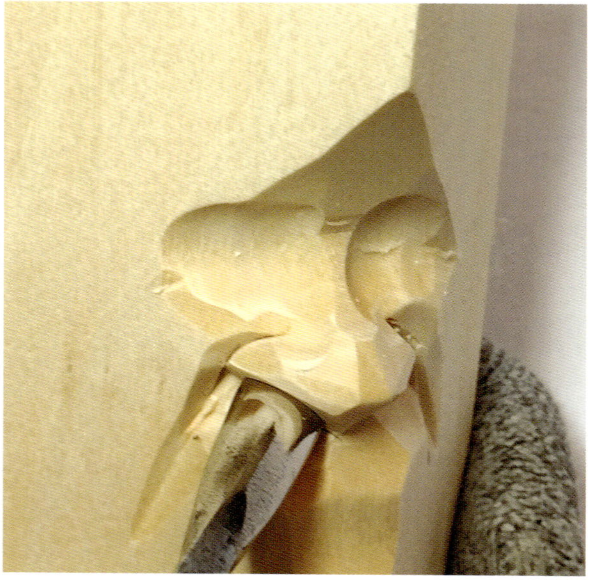

14 Establish the nostrils. Using a small gouge turned upside down, push straight into the wood, not upward. You can pop the chip out by taking the tip of your knife and carefully pushing the chip downward. It will break the chip, but that's OK.

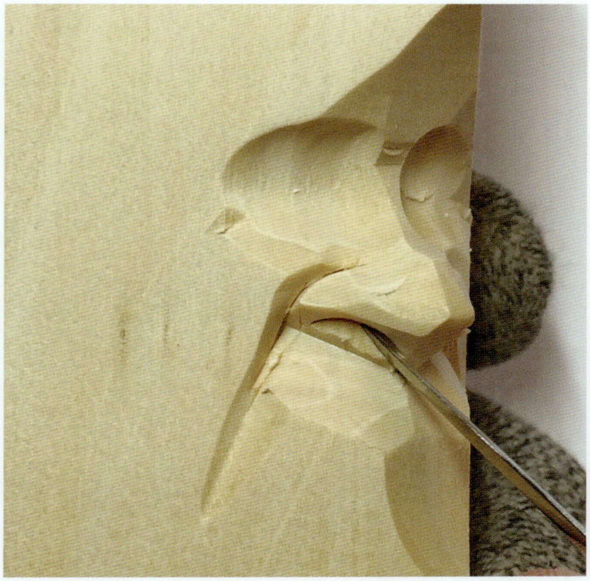

15 With the knife, cut inward in the first step of a triangle.

16 Make the second cut of the triangle.

17 Remove the chip, finishing the triangle. The deepest point should be right in the center of the chip.

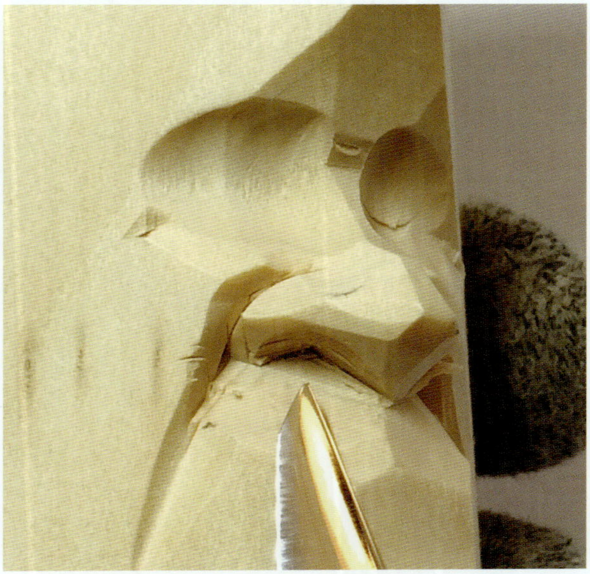

18 Progress! Make careful cuts to remove the "fuzzies." Notice that the triangle makes the opening look deeper. From this point, you could make the nose longer by removing more wood from the bridge of the nose if desired.

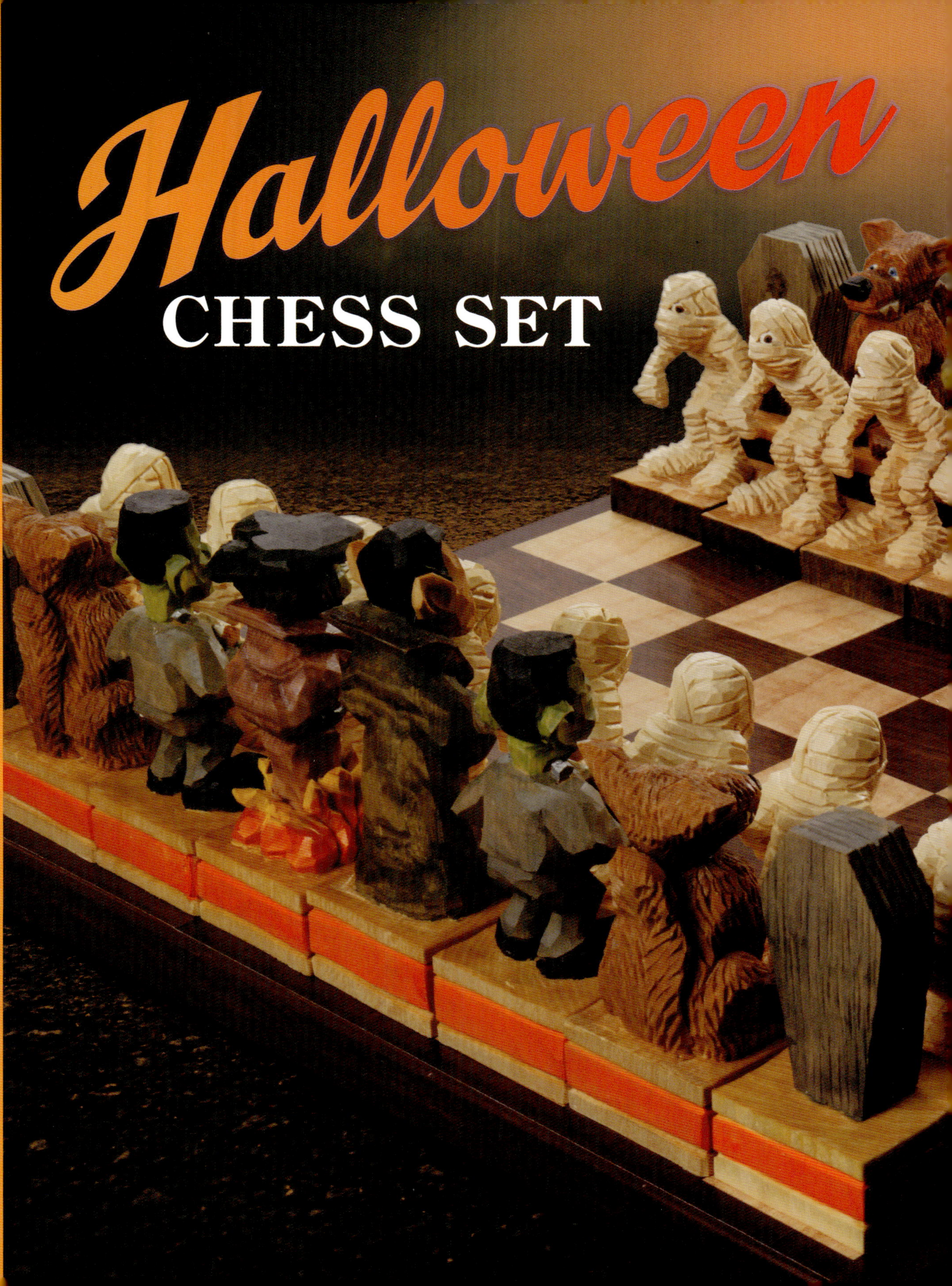
Halloween
CHESS SET

As a child, I always liked fall best, with its cooler weather and, most importantly, Halloween. Thoughts of Halloween costumes and candy were never far from my mind. The endless parade of monsters walking up and down the streets, looking to grab all the sugar they could before having to return home, was a magical event. I found myself planning my Halloween tactics weeks ahead of time.

As an adult, however, I find that my neighbors don't like when I knock on their doors, dressed up and wanting candy, on Halloween. Apparently, when you're 6 feet tall and 40-something years old, it's not as cute. We can, however, relive the magical adventures of our youth with a little imagination. My imagination led me to carve this Halloween chess set, where a few of my favorite monsters take to the streets of battle for the best candy.

Paint Colors

The author used these products for the projects. Substitute your choices of brands and colors as desired.

Apple Barrel

- Black (matte)
- Black Metallic (metallic)
- Blue Bonnet (matte)
- Bright Red (matte)
- Bright Yellow (matte)
- Brown Oxide (matte)
- Harvest Orange (matte)
- Nutmeg Brown (matte)
- Pewter Grey (matte)
- Pumpkin Orange (matte) (note: this swatch is with the Christmas colors)
- Purple (matte)
- Satin Cream (matte)
- White (matte)

DecoArt

- Shimmering Silver (metallic)

FolkArt

- Clover (matte)

Minwax

- Honeycomb (water-based stain)

Halloween Pawn

The pawns in a chess set are the most numerous, and they usually do most of the work. When I was planning which piece would be the pawn, I thought in terms of "most." Then it hit me: the sands of Egypt hold the secrets of many mummies, with new ones still being discovered. The mummy pawn was dreamed into reality.

This pattern is easier than it looks; however, you have sixteen pawns to carve. Either pace yourself for the journey of carving them all at once, or sit back and carve a few here and there between your other chess pieces. Either way, don't get "wrapped up" in the numbers game, as once the mummies are done, you're halfway finished with the chess set.

1 With the pattern cut out, mark the arms, feet, head, and abdomen area. I used the ⅜" (10mm) soft V-tool to block out the areas because I like the softer cuts that this tool creates in the low areas.

2 With your favorite carving knife, shape the carving. This guy is a mummy, so you don't need to get too carried away with detail; just round the limbs and head and be sure to remove all saw marks.

3 With the same knife, separate the legs and clean up the base.

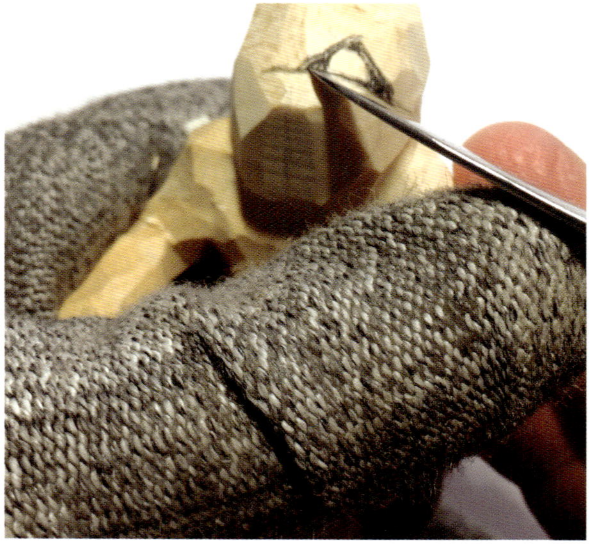

4 Make the basic eye (see page 10) by drawing a triangle with a circle inside. Then, with the detail knife, remove the three triangles in the corners created by the circle. Remember that you have eight mummies to carve for each side. I chose to do four with eyes on the left and four with eyes on the right.

5 With the ¼" (6mm) 45° V-tool, establish the bandages that wrap around the body. I do not mark the layout with a pencil, as I find that it looks better when done freehand. Lay the V-tool on its side (see sidebar on page 8) and use it like a chisel to create a sense of overlap. I start on the head and work my way down the body to the feet.

6 Finish up the carving by making sure there are no hanging chips. Clean up the bandages and add any final details.

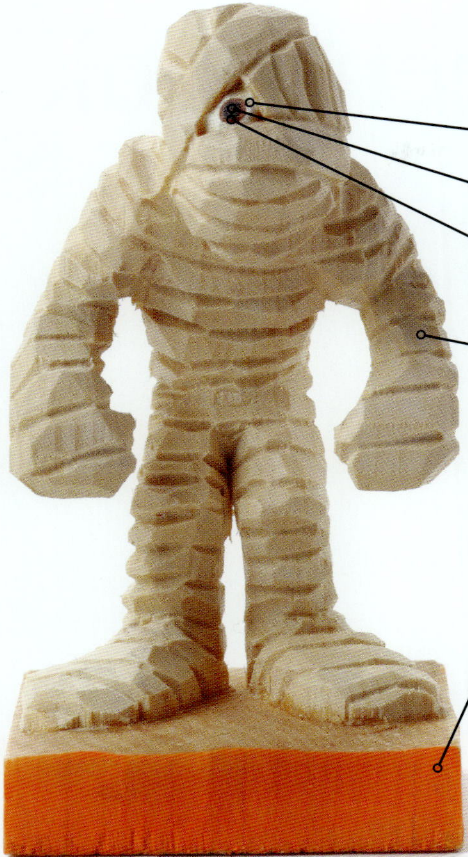

Pawn Paint Key

White 100%

Black 100%

Nutmeg Brown 100%

Satin Cream 50/50

Pumpkin Orange 50/50 or Black 50/50*

100% = full-strength
50/50 = 50% paint 50% water, mixed
* Side 1 bases = Pumpkin Orange 50/50
Side 2 bases = Black 50/50

Front

Side

Back

Halloween Rook

The rook in chess looks like a castle, so I started to think about landmarks and where castles are located. In designing the Halloween rook, I thought of spooky places to visit and found myself considering my "final destination"—thus, the coffin was my choice.

The coffin is a super-easy carving, and carving the rooks after the pawns is a welcome reward after all of those wraps. Nice, crisp cuts will have the coffins ready to host their new owners in no time at all on the chess battlefield.

1 Use your favorite carving knife to remove all saw marks. Don't forget the base.

2 With the ¼" (6mm) 45° V-tool, carve the cross by laying the tool on its side like a chisel to relieve the areas around it.

3 With the ¼" (6mm) 45° V-tool, carve the wood texture by cutting vertical lines. I cut shorter lines in between the long ones so it looks more natural.

4 With the ¼" (6mm) 45° V-tool, carve lines to create the front and back lid. Then create the wood grain on the sides and back of the piece as you did in step 3.

5 With the same V-tool, carve two lines around the base to add a bit of interest.

Rook Paint Key

- Pewter Grey 50/50
- Black 50/50
- Pumpkin Orange 50/50 or Black 50/50*

100% = full-strength
50/50 = 50% paint 50% water, mixed
* Side 1 bases = Pumpkin Orange 50/50
  Side 2 bases = Black 50/50

Front

Back

Side

Halloween Knight

The knights in chess are always represented as horses. I've always thought this odd until I came to realize the importance of the figure and the humor I could get from using a werewolf as the knight in this Halloween chess set.

No bones about it—this guy has a lot of fur! Treat the fur as the last step, and you'll be howling with excitement about carving this piece.

1 With the pattern cut out, mark out the legs, head, tail, and ears. I used the ⅜" (10mm) soft V-tool to block out these areas. I like the softer cuts that the soft V-tool creates in the low areas.

2 With your carving knife, carve away all of the saw marks and shape the corners of the legs, ears, tail, body, and head.

3 With the ¼" (6mm) 45° V-tool, establish the separation of the legs, tail, and feet. Don't try to carve through the legs to the other side. A crisp line is all you need.

4 With the same V-tool, carve the eyes (see page 10), nose (see page 11), and mouth. Clean up any chips with the knife.

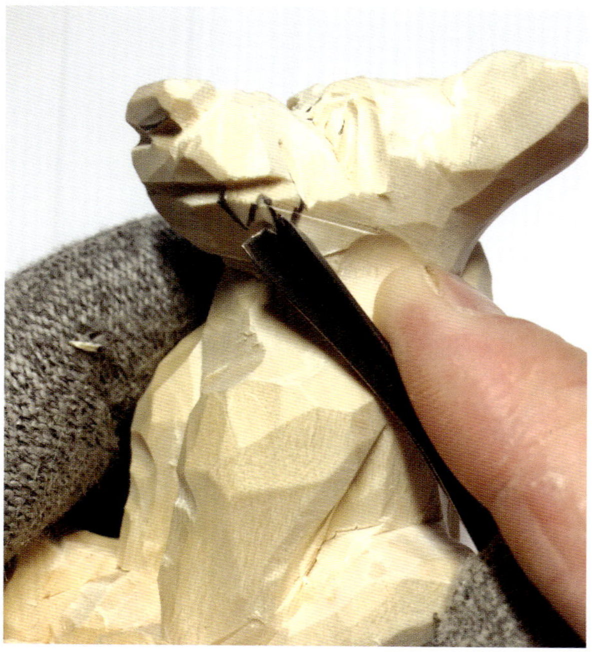

5 With the mouth carved, draw in the teeth and ear details. Carve these areas with the ¼" (6mm) 45° V-tool laying on its side like a chisel (see sidebar on page 8).

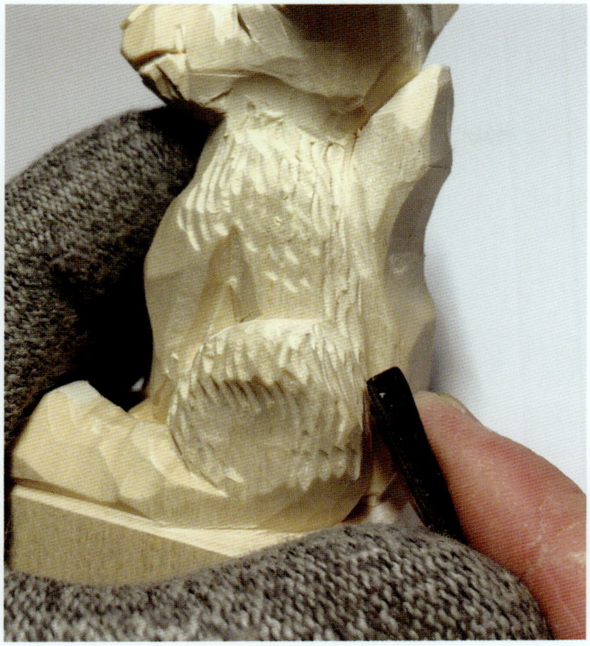

6 With the same V-tool, carve the fur texture. This is time consuming but well worth it. Pay attention to the way that the fur will lie on the piece. Do not draw in the fur, as your carving will get messy quickly. Make short cuts, around 1⁄16" (2mm) to ⅛" (3mm) long.

7 With the fur texture carved, take the time to remove any hanging chips with the carving knife and add final details.

8 With the ¼" (6mm) 45° V-tool, carve two lines around the base to add a bit of interest.

Front

Knight Paint Key

- Black 100%
- Blue Bonnet 100%
- White 100%
- Brown Oxide 50/50
- Black 100%
- Pumpkin Orange 50/50 or Black 50/50*

100% = full-strength
50/50 = 50% paint 50% water, mixed
* Side 1 bases = Pumpkin Orange 50/50
Side 2 bases = Black 50/50

Side

Back

Halloween Bishop

In my mind, the bishop in chess is the wise recordkeeper. I found humor in making Frankenstein my recordkeeper. With a borrowed mind and loosely sewn arms, how could anything go wrong?

"Frank" is a joy to carve; however, he has a few tricky spots. Pay close attention to how the book sits against the body and how it comes out below the arms. Before you know it, Frank will be keeping records on how many chess pieces you have left to carve.

1 Establish where the book will be. The arms and hands all wrap around this first step. With the ⅜" (10mm) soft V-tool, carve the book and outline the arms.

2 Following the angle of the book, use your favorite carving knife to carve the arms to match. Stop short of the shoulder, as the angle changes in that area. Next, block out the arms, legs, and feet with the soft V-tool. Use the carving knife to shape the side of the face.

3 With the carving knife, cut inward to shape the bottom of the book.

4 With the same knife, establish where the nose and eyes will go.

5 Continue shaping the nose and adding the nostrils. Refer to the Carving Noses section, beginning on page 11.

6 With the ¾" (19mm) #7 gouge, narrow the face at the temple area, continuing around toward the ear. Carve the opposite side as well. Shape the back sides of the ears with a V-tool.

7 With the V-tool lying on its side like a chisel (see sidebar on page 8), establish the hairline. This creates the layer of hair and narrows the face at the same time. Also carve the book pages with the ¼" (6mm) 45° V-tool.

8 With the carving knife, carve the bolts in the neck. Carve from square to octagon, then round.

9 With the ⅛" (3mm) 45° V-tool, carve the eyes (refer to Carving Eyes on page 10), hair texture, mouth, and hands.

10 With the carving knife, finish carving between the legs and then clean up the base. Make any final tweaks to the clothing, such as separating the pants from the shirt in the back, with the V-tool.

11 With the ¼" (6mm) 45° V-tool, carve two lines around the base to add a bit of interest. Take the time to clean up any hanging chips.

Bishop Paint Key

- Black 50/50
- Blue Bonnet 100%
- White 100%
- Black 100%
- Shimmering Silver 100%
- Clover 50/50
- Nutmeg Brown 50/50
- Pewter Grey 50/50
- Pumpkin Orange 50/50 or Black 50/50*

100% = full-strength
50/50 = 50% paint 50% water, mixed
* Side 1 bases = Pumpkin Orange 50/50
Side 2 bases = Black 50/50

Front

Side

Back

Halloween King

Designing the king didn't require much thought: Dracula is the king of Halloween! Although capturing the king can be tricky in chess, this carving is not. With this simple straight-on approach, and because you don't have to carve hands, you'll be batty over how fun this guy is.

1 With the pattern cut out, draw in the head and arms. With the ⅜" (10mm) soft V-tool, block out these areas.

2 With your favorite carving knife, round the body and carve the separation in the cloak. Remove all saw marks from the piece. Shape the face with the knife by carving both sides of the face to a point toward the nose.

3 With the same knife, carve the arms so that they wrap around the body.

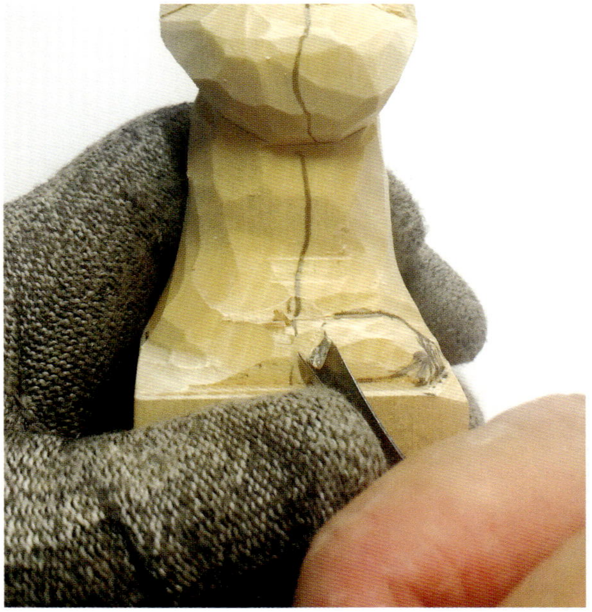

4 Draw in the cloak lines and the exposed shoe. Shape the shoe with the ¼" (6mm) 45° V-tool. Clean up with the carving knife.

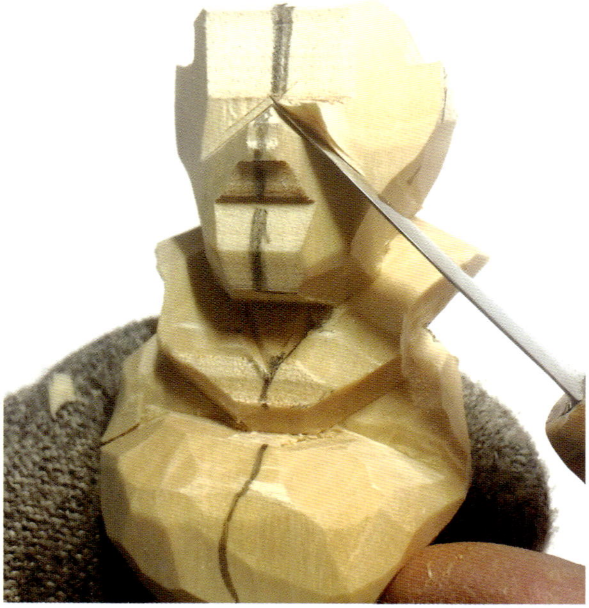

5 With the carving knife, establish the top of the nose and eye sockets.

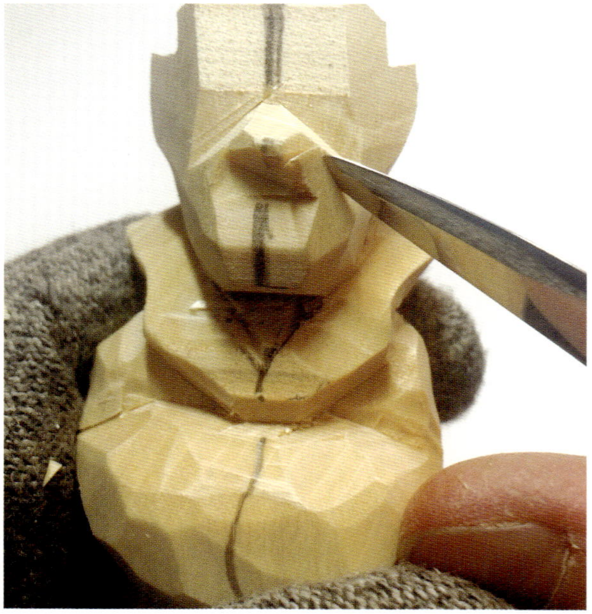

6 Continue carving the nose. Refer to the Carving Noses section, starting on page 11.

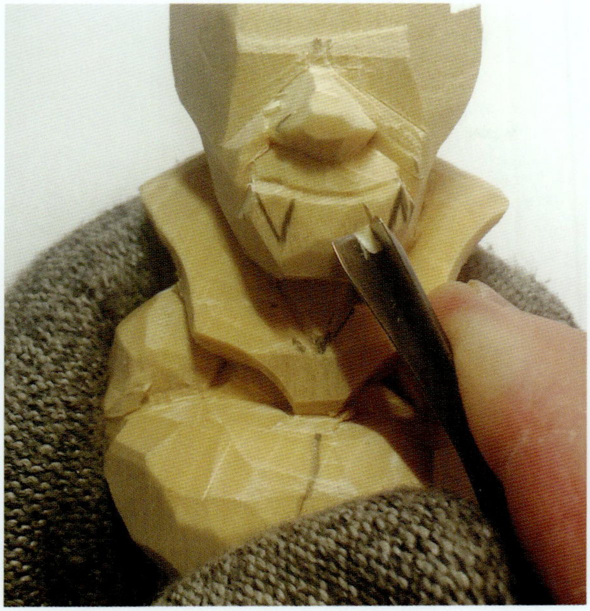

7 With the ¼" (6mm) 45° V-tool, carve the mouth. Draw in the fangs (teeth) and then carve them by laying the V-tool on its side like a chisel.

8 With the carving knife, carve above the eyebrows, narrowing the forehead. Shape the head and then the ears, making sure that each has a point at the top.

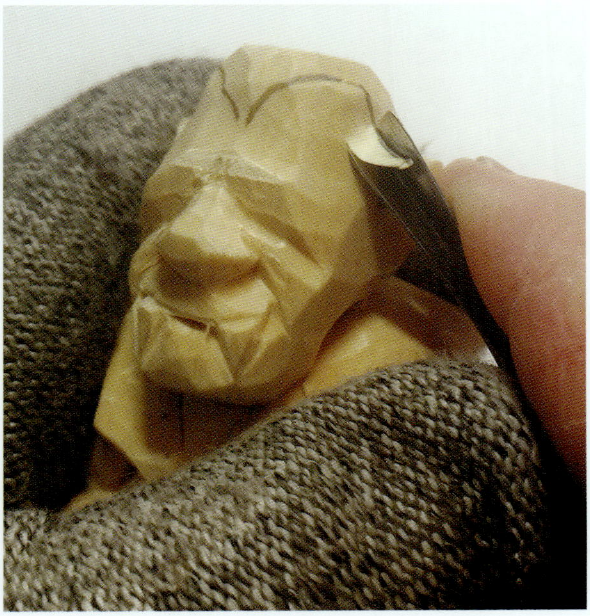

9 Remember that Dracula has a large widow's peak, so draw that in and then carve the hair texture with the V-tool lying on its side. Also with the V-tool, separate the cloak below the chin at the upper chest. Carve the cloak separation, the body, and the sleeves.

10 With the ⅛" (3mm) 45° V-tool, carve the eyes (see Carving Eyes, page 10).

11 With the same V-tool, carve the collar details.

12 With the ¼" (6mm) 45° V-tool, carve two lines around the base to add a bit of interest.

King Paint Key

- Black 100%
- Blue Bonnet 100%
- White 100%
- Honeycomb 50/50
- Red 100%
- Black 50/50 (Cloak)
- Mixture of 1 part Black Metallic 50/50 and 1 part Red 50/50
- Pumpkin Orange 50/50 or Black 50/50*

100% = full-strength
50/50 = 50% paint 50% water, mixed
* Side 1 bases = Pumpkin Orange 50/50
  Side 2 bases = Black 50/50

Front

Side

Back

Halloween Queen

When I was thinking about the queen piece for the set, the witch was an easy choice—in part because there is a limited number of recognizable female monsters, and in part because of the fear that witches bring to Halloween. With this fear, along with the power that the queen has in chess, the witch rising from the flames was born.

Given that the queen is the most powerful piece on the board, she deserved a piece that was a bit of a challenge to carve. Don't get burned by rushing into this piece; you need to take it slow. Pay close attention to how the hair and face are layered, as this area has a few tight spots. Also, map out the fire beforehand to create different levels of flame height.

1 With the pattern cut out, draw in the head, hat, fire, and arms. With the ⅜" (10mm) soft V-tool, block out these areas. Next, use the same tool to shape the face by carving the sides off, back toward where the ears would be.

2 With the ¼" (6mm) 45° V-tool, cut in the details for the hair, collar, and belt.

3 With your carving knife, carve the hard lines under the chest and between the arms.

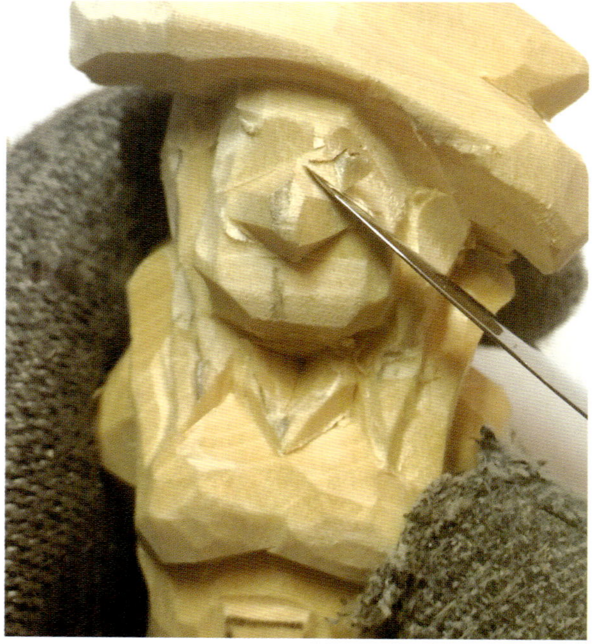

4 With the knife, shape the nose and eye area. Make indents for the eyes and begin to give the nose a knobbly shape (see Carving Noses, starting on page 11).

5 With the knife, shape the chin area and clean up the collar area from the hairline.

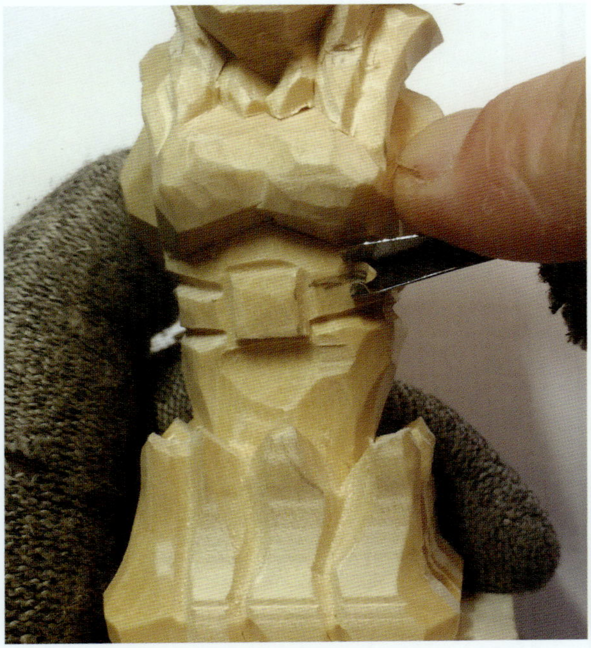

6 With the ⅛" (3mm) 45° V-tool, carve the smile line, mouth, and belt details, and separate the fire details.

7 With the the same V-tool, carve the eyes (refer to Carving Eyes on page 10). Clean up the eyes with your detail knife.

8 With the ⅛" (3mm) #9 gouge, carve the hair texture and establish the belt buckle.

9 With the carving knife, carve the individual flames and clean up the base.

10 With the ¼" (6mm) 45° V-tool, carve the hat, adding a few wrinkles.

11 With the same V-tool, carve two lines around the base to add a bit of interest.

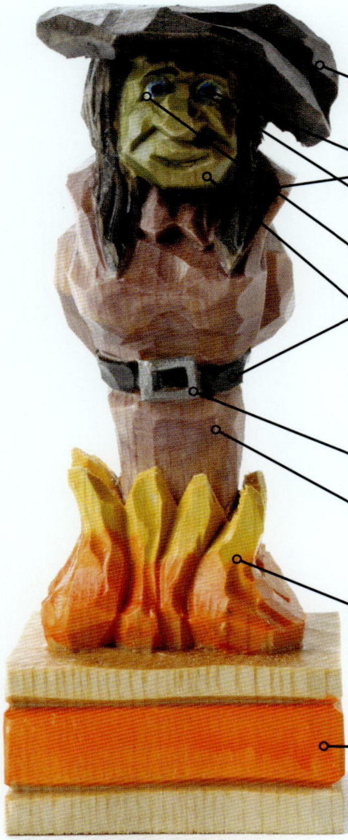

Front

Queen Paint Key

- Black 50/50
- Black 100%
- Blue Bonnet 100%
- White 100%
- Clover 50/50
- Shimmering Silver 100%
- Purple 50/50
- Mixture of 1 part Harvest Orange 50/50 and 1 part Yellow 50/50
- Pumpkin Orange 50/50 or Black 50/50*

100% = full-strength
50/50 = 50% paint 50% water, mixed
* Side 1 bases = Pumpkin Orange 50/50
Side 2 bases = Black 50/50

Side

Back

Patterns

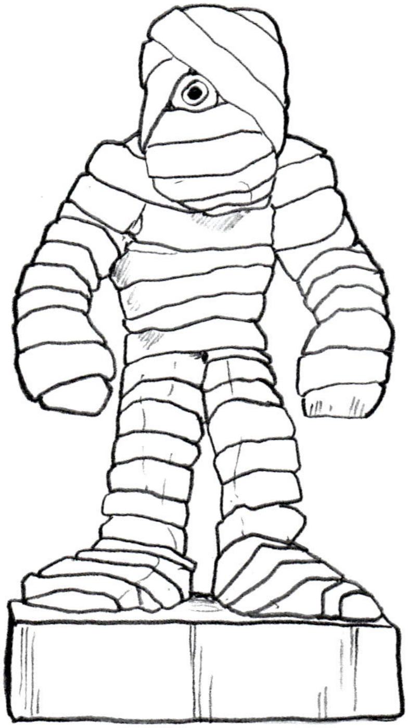

Halloween Pawn
Front

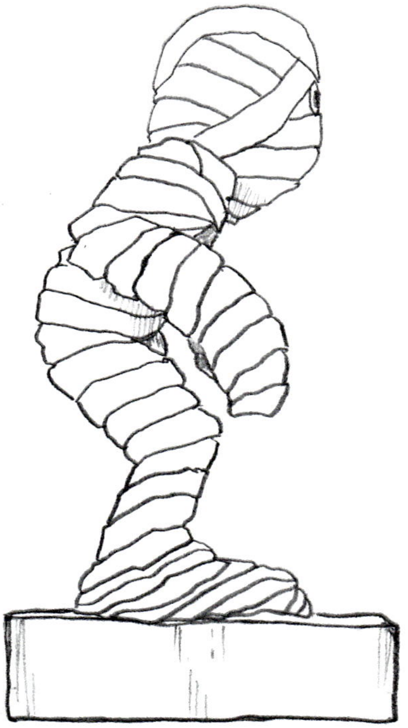

Halloween Pawn
Side

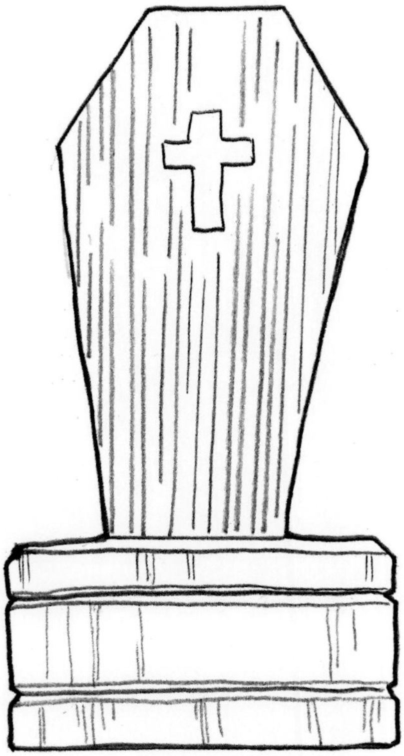

Halloween Rook
Front

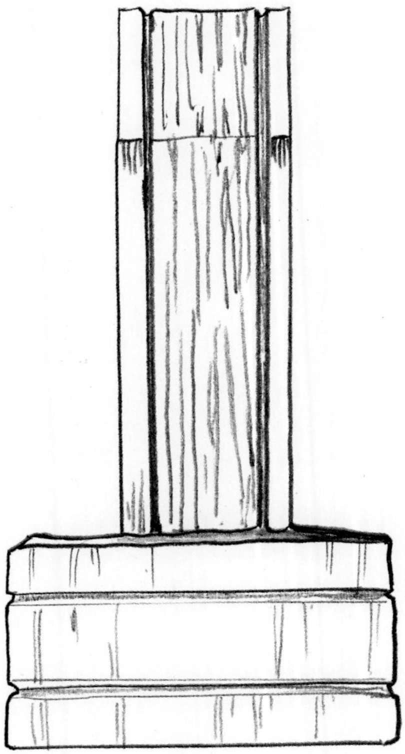

Halloween Rook
Side

Halloween Knight
Front

Halloween Knight
Side

Halloween Bishop
Front

Halloween Bishop
Side

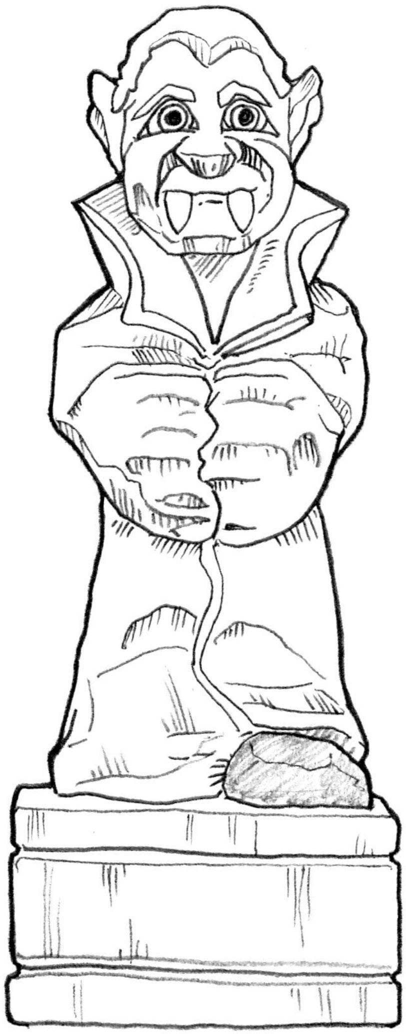

Halloween King
Front

Halloween King
Side

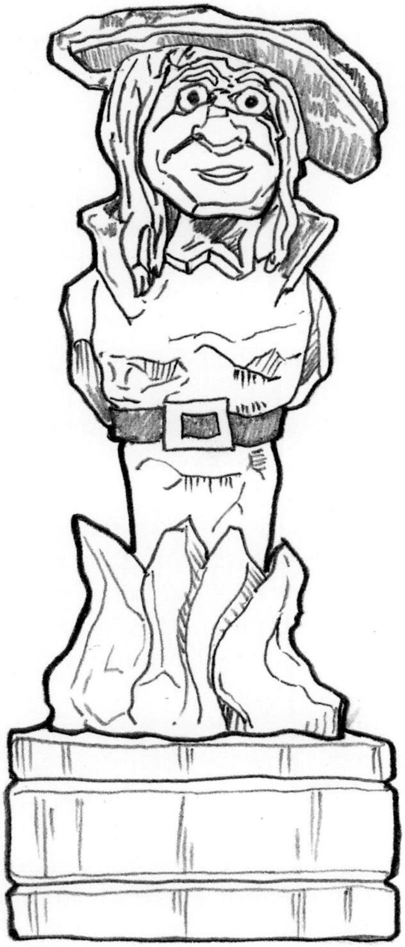

Halloween Queen
Front

Halloween Queen
Side

About the Author

DWAYNE GOSNELL grew up in a small town in North Carolina, dreaming of the day when he would go off into the world and make his mark. In his childhood, he would often help his father with woodworking projects, and he enjoyed the process of creating something from nothing. It wasn't until later in life, after serving in the Marine Corps, that he was thrown back into creating. He happened into a local woodworking shop and purchased a book about carving faces into walking sticks. After two visits to the emergency room, dozens of boxes of bandages, and countless trips back to the woodworking shop for more books, the man behind the counter said with a grin, "You know we have a carving club, right?" The man gave Dwayne information about the Catawba Valley Woodcarvers and told him to bring some carvings for "show and tell."

At Dwayne's first meeting, he walked into the crowded stockroom carrying a bag filled with two tools, some carving books, and a dozen tree limbs with butchered faces carved into them. He sat alone in the back and thought, *There's no way I'm opening this bag of junk in front of these master carvers.* With the life-sized birds and amazing caricatures the others had brought, Dwayne was overwhelmed.

When he heard a female voice say "hi," he looked and saw Paige Cartledge. Little did he know that it would start a conversation that fueled his fire for caricature carving. Paige's husband, Mitch, agreed to teach Dwayne a thing or two...or a lot. Dwayne carved with Mitch on Monday nights for almost a year, and he became addicted to everything caricature. Even though he wasn't good at it yet, he had an amazing teacher and was determined to absorb everything about caricature carving.

Fast-forward more than a decade, and now Dwayne is the guy who's sharing what he's learned and how to avoid the mistakes he's made. He is president of the Catawba Valley Woodcarvers and teaches classes around the United States. He owns rough-out patterns for the Phil and Vicki Bishop Collection as well as most of Steve Brown's rough-out collection. In February 2020, he was inducted into the Caricature Carvers of America.

Dwayne lives in Hickory, North Carolina, with his wife, Melissa, and his two children, Payton and Mason. He works in law enforcement, and carving has always been a way for him to unwind after a long day. Throughout the years, what started as a hobby has become an endless passion to create. He has won many awards, but the friendships he has made are worth far more than any of them.

For more information, visit Dwayne's website, *dgosnellwoodcarving.com*.